in the
Injeel

Fouad Masri

Adha in the Injeel

© 2004 by Fouad Masri

All rights reserved.
No part of this publication may be reproduced in any form without written permission from the publisher: Fouad Masri/Cedar Cross Media, P.O. Box 60986, Indianapolis, IN 46250. www.unlockthetruth.net.

ISBN: 978-1-944590-09-3

Layout Design by Wesleyan Publishing House.
Cover Art by Alesa Bahler / Legacy Design.

All Scripture quotations, unless otherwise indicated, are taken from the Holy Bible, New International Version®, NIV® Copyright © 1973, 1978, 1984 by Biblica, Inc.® Used by permission. All rights reserved worldwide.

Quotations from the Qur'an are taken from The Quran Translation, 7th Edition, by Abdullah Yusuf Ali (Elmhurst, NY: Tahrike Tarsile Quran, Inc., 2001).

Printed in the United States of America.

uslims around the world annually celebrate the feast of Al-Adha. This feast takes place on the 10th of Dhul-Hijat, a month in the Muslim lunar calendar.

The root word for *Adha* is the Arabic word *Dahiya*, which means *sacrifice*. The Al-Adha feast is also known as the Feast of Sacrifice or the Great Feast, Id Al-Kabir. In the Turkic world the Adha feast is known as Qurbani.

At the Al-Adha feast many Muslims sacrifice a sheep or a ram to commemorate the holy event when God redeemed the son of Abraham. This incident is recorded in the Qur'an in Sura 37:99-111.

The Jewish religion also believes in this same holy event when God redeemed the son of Abraham with a ram. When Abraham was about to sacrifice his son, the angel of the Lord stopped him. Abraham looked and saw a ram caught in the thicket by its horns.

He took the ram and sacrificed it as a burnt offering. The full record of this event is found in the Tawrat, the Book of Genesis 22:1-19.

Although the Jewish religion does not commemorate this specific event with a feast, the same idea and meaning are included in the Passover that was given to them by the prophet Moses. Jews celebrate the Passover to commemorate the night when God spared the Jewish firstborn from being slain in Egypt. The angel of death passed over the houses of those who put the blood of a slaughtered sheep at their doorposts, without harming their firstborn. The Passover is recorded in the Tawrat, the Book of Exodus 12:1-14.

Where is the Christian Adha?

Since Christians believe in both the Passover and the Adha events, why don't they celebrate them? Is there a Christian Passover too? To answer these questions, we need to look in the *Injeel* (the New Testament) and examine its teachings on the character of God and His plan for humankind.

1. THE INJEEL TEACHES THAT **GOD IS LOVE**

God is the Creator of the universe and seeks fellowship with his creation. God's joy and pleasure is to communicate with humans, the highest of creation, bestowed with both a mind and a will.

The Injeel says:

> "God is love. Whoever lives in love lives in God, and God in him." 1 John 4:16

> "I [Jesus] have come that they may have life, and have it to the full." John 10:10

Since God seeks fellowship with humans, why is our world so far from God? Why do people feel separated from God? It seems as if a great gulf separates us from enjoying God and His love.

2 THE INJEEL TEACHES THAT **GOD IS HOLY**

God is holy and righteous, and humans are sinful. Everywhere we turn, we see the sinfulness of humans. Their actions are symptoms of the real disease of Sin. Sin is rebellion against God.

All humans have sinned. Sin is choosing our way instead of God's way. All humans fall short of perfectly obeying God's standard and law. Since the days of Adam, all people have chosen to go their own way rather than to obey God. This disobedience is what the Injeel calls sin.

We have all sinned against God Almighty and cannot remove our guilt. A righteous God is holy and cannot fellowship with sinful people.

The Injeel affirms that all have sinned against a holy God:

> *"There is no one righteous, not even one. There is none who understands; no one who seeks God. All have turned away; they have together become worthless; there is no one who does good, not even one."* Romans 3:10-12
>
> *"For all have sinned and fall short of the glory of God."* Romans 3:23

HOLY GOD

SIN

SINFUL HUMANS

3 THE INJEEL TEACHES THAT GOD IS JUST

The Injeel continues to explain that sin is what separates us from our loving and holy God. God's holiness condemns sin. The very righteous character of God cannot accept sin. Therefore, God and humans are separated by a great gulf, which is sin.

This separation from God results in spiritual death.

The Injeel says:

> *"The wages of sin is death."* Romans 6:23

The wages of sin is death, yet no sinner can die to redeem someone else. This makes a great gulf between Holy God and sinful men and women.

Humans need God the way a lightbulb needs electricity. A lightbulb without electricity is dead, lifeless, and aimless. Sin has separated humans from God and made us spiritually dead, lifeless, and aimless.

God's justice compels Him to punish and destroy sin. We have sinned against God Almighty, and the penalty is death. God cannot forgive a sinful person until that sinful person's debt is paid. Mere good works, such as fasting or giving alms to the poor, cannot pay the debt by earning God's favor. Even the most noble acts fall short of God's perfect holiness and justice. Our best is not good enough to please a perfect God, which means every single person – even the best of us – has sinned and must be punished.

A criminal cannot redeem another criminal; simply put, all humans have sinned and have fallen short of God's law. God's holiness and justice do not allow forgiveness without payment of this huge debt. We have chosen our own way and have broken God's commandment, so we must pay the penalty. That penalty is separation from God.

4 THE INJEEL TEACHES THAT GOD IS MERCIFUL

God's mercy sought to provide an answer to this problem. God wants to fellowship with us, his creation, but sin has created a gulf between him and us. Only a righteous person can cross over the gulf to God. However, we have already established that everyone has sinned and has fallen short!

Everyone, that is, except Jesus Christ. The Injeel teaches that Jesus Christ is the only bridge between a holy God and sinful humans. **Why Jesus and not anyone else?**

Miraculous Birth

The Injeel teaches that Jesus Christ was not the son of a human father but was conceived by the power of the Holy Spirit in the womb of the virgin Mary. He was the only person to be born of a virgin. Jesus Christ's birth was not a result of the will of man but the will of God.

Jesus Christ is unique in His miraculous birth. No prophet or leader has been born from a virgin. All prophets claimed they were just humans, while Jesus Christ claimed he was the *Word of God, Kalimat Allah*. God's power is responsible for this miracle.

> *"But the angel said to her: 'Do not be afraid, Mary, you have found favor with God. You will be with child and give birth to a son, and you will give him the name Jesus. He will be great and will be called the Son of the Most High. The Lord God will give Him the throne of His father David, and he will reign over the house of Jacob forever; his kingdom will never end.' 'How can this be,' Mary asked the angel, 'since I am a virgin?' The angel answered, 'The Holy Spirit will come upon you, and the power of the Most High will overshadow you. So the holy one to be born will be called the Son of God. Even Elizabeth your relative is going to have a child in her old age, and she who was said to be barren is in her sixth month. For nothing is impossible with God'"* Luke 1:30-37

Miraculous Life

Jesus Christ lived a life of purity and honesty. He was obedient to the laws of God throughout His life. Jesus Christ taught like no one else and miraculously healed every weakness and disease. He was sinless from birth and was considered the greatest teacher who ever lived.

> *"Jesus went throughout Galilee, teaching in their synagogues, preaching the good news of the kingdom, and healing every disease and sickness among the people. News about him spread all over Syria, and people brought to him all who were ill with various diseases, those suffering severe pain, the demon-possessed, the epileptics and the paralytics, and he healed them. Large crowds from Galilee, Decapolis, Jerusalem, Judea, and the region across Jordan followed him."*
>
> Matthew 4:23-25

Miraculous Death

Jesus Christ did not come to earth merely to be a good teacher or healer. He came to be the sacrifice of God. Because Jesus Christ is righteous, sinless from birth, his death alone can pay the penalty for sin. He came to redeem humanity from its fallen state. The Injeel clearly states that all have sinned against God and need salvation. Salvation means to be pardoned by God because someone paid the penalty we could not pay ourselves.

Jesus Christ, the only righteous one, willingly paid the debt we owe. Humans are dead in sin. Sin is the gulf that separates us from God. Jesus Christ was crucified and died as a righteous sacrifice for the human race. Just as Abraham sacrificed a ram instead of his son, Jesus'death on the cross was the sacrifice to pay the penalty of the sin of all humankind. The sheep died so that the son of Abraham could be set free. Likewise, Jesus died so that we can be set free. For as God redeemed the son of Abraham with a ram, likewise God redeemed the world through Jesus Christ.

As Muslims sacrifice a sheep at Al-Adha and the Israelites sacrificed a sheep during

Passover in Egypt, God made Jesus Christ the perfect sacrifice for our sins.

Jesus became the true Adha. He was the Lamb of God to lift away the sins of the world. John the Baptist (known as the prophet Yahya) prophesied when he saw Jesus and said:

> "Behold, the Lamb of God who takes away the sin of the world!"   John 1:29

Through Jesus Christ, God bridged the gulf that separated us from Him.

> "All this is from God, who reconciled us to himself through Christ and gave us the ministry of reconciliation."   2 Corinthians 5:18

The justice of God was satisfied, for the penalty of sin was paid. The mercy of God was satisfied, for humans have redemption.

Miraculous Resurrection

Jesus Christ paid the penalty for our sin so that we can have fellowship with God.

Jesus Christ is righteous and did not deserve death. He is the *Word of God*, Kalimat Allah. Jesus is the incarnate Word of God becoming the sacrifice for our salvation.

Christ rose from the dead on the third day according to prophecy. Christ's resurrection proved that His sacrifice was acceptable to God.

> *"For what I received I passed on to you as of first importance; that Christ died for our sins according to the Scriptures, that He was buried, that He was raised on the third day according to the Scriptures, and that he appeared to Peter, and then to the Twelve. After that he appeared to more than five hundred of the brothers at the same time; most of them are still living, though some have fallen asleep."* 1 Corinthians 15:3-6

Christians around the world celebrate the Adha and the Passover in one glorious celebration of the crucifixion and resurrection of Jesus Christ (known in English as *Easter* and in Arabic as *Id Al-Qiama*). This is the Adha and Passover come true!

These holy events were object lessons God used so that we could understand true redemption. The Bible says that the blood of calves and sheep will not wash away sins and that all our good works are like filthy rags compared to God's righteousness. No one can possibly pay the huge debt that is owed to God.

The good news is that God sent Jesus Christ to be the sacrificial Lamb of God who takes the sins of the world.

Jesus Christ Is Our True Adha!

Let's say a friend of mine asks me to watch his house while he travels and I accidentally destroy the furniture. However, before his return, I wash his car. Would that cover the cost of replacing the furniture? No! If I ask my friend to have mercy and forgive me for destroying his furniture since I washed the car, is it acceptable? No!

Even if he forgave me, my friend still has to pay for new furniture. Likewise, our good works are not righteous enough compared to God's righteousness. Our good works will never erase sin, for we are expected to do good and obey God's commandments.

Our sin insults God's righteousness; only Jesus' sacrificial work can suffice. Only the Christian Adha covers the debt of our sin and bridges the gap.

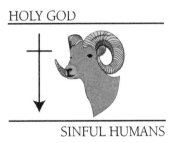

The Christian Adha is available to everyone, for Christ came to save all people, of all nations and races. Through Christ we can cross over to fellowship with God and experience His love and redemption.

5 THE INJEEL TEACHES THAT
GOD IS FORGIVING

It is not enough to know that God has found an *Adha* for sin. Each one of us needs to receive this sacrifice in a personal and humble decision.

We experience God's forgiveness in the following way. We must repent of our sin and receive Jesus Christ as Lord and Savior in order to experience God's love and forgiveness.

Repentance is turning to God from our own sinful ways and receiving God's offer of forgiveness, made possible by Christ's work on the cross (the Christian Adha).

The Injeel says:

> *"If we confess our sins, he is faithful and just to forgive our sins and cleanse us from all unrighteousness"*   1 John 1:9

- God forgives our sins if we confess them because Christ paid the debt.
- The perfect justice of God demanded punishment.
- The mercy of God was shown in the Christian Adha.
- Forgiveness can be granted because the justice of God was satisfied.
- Forgiveness can be enjoyed by repentant sinners because Christ paid the debt.

Sin dwells within the heart of every human being. The human race is in need of a "heart transplant," a new life that will change a sinner to a saint.

The Injeel says:

> "The wages of sin is death, but the gift of God is eternal life in Christ Jesus our Lord"   Romans 6:23

The Christian Adha released us from spiritual death and offered us eternal life. God's gift of eternal life is in accepting Christ's sacrifice for our sin. We receive Christ's sacrifice by faith (trust).

Christ's sacrifice is free yet priceless. We must receive it by faith. We can do nothing to earn it ourselves.

> *"For it is by grace you have been saved, through faith – and this is not from yourselves, it is the gift of God – not by works, so that no one can boast."*
>
> Ephesians 2:8-9

The gift of God cannot be enjoyed unless it is received. We receive Christ and His sacrificial work by a personal commitment.

> *"Yet to all who received him, to those believed in his name, he gave the right to become children of God – children born not of natural descent, nor of human decision or a husband's will, but born of God."*
>
> John 1:12-13

Christ is seeking to enter our lives, cleanse us from sin, and mend our broken relationship with God. Christ wants to be our Lord and Savior. Jesus says in the Injeel:

> *"Here I am! I stand at the door and knock. If any one hears My voice and opens the door, I will come in."*
>
> Revelation 3:20

Prayer is talking to God. We can pray to God wherever we are and whenever we want. To receive Christ's sacrifice (the Christian Adha), we are to pray to God and know by faith (by trusting God) that we have salvation.

Your prayer to God can be something like this:

> **Dear Lord, thank You for Your love for me. I ask Your forgiveness because of Christ's atoning death. I open the door of my life and receive Jesus Christ as my Lord and Savior. Make me a new person. Thank You for giving me eternal life. In Jesus' name.   Amen**

Pray this prayer and ask Christ to enter your life, forgive your sins, and restore your fellowship with God. If you sincerely asked Christ to enter your life, be assured that He did.

It is important to know that God's promises are true. In Revelation 3:20 Christ says, *"I stand at the door and knock, if anyone hears my voice and opens the door, I will come in."* If you opened the door of your life and asked Christ to enter as Savior and Lord, He will not deceive you. Christ is faithful.

The Injeel teaches that Jesus Christ is faithful to His promises:

> *"If you remain in me and my words remain in you, ask whatever you wish, and it will be given to you."*
> John 15:7

> *"Never will I leave you; never will I forsake you."*
> Hebrews 13:5

> *"Jesus Christ is the same yesterday and today and forever."*
> Hebrews 13:8

> *"I know whom I have believed, and am convinced that he is able to guard what I have entrusted to him for that day."*
> 2 Timothy 1:12

> *"being confident of this, that he who began a good work in you will carry it on to completion until the day of Christ Jesus."*
> Philippians 1:6

Points For Growth

Receiving Christ as your Savior and Lord isthe beginning of a great journey with God. Below is an easy reminder to assist you inyour daily spiritual growth and help you experience God's great love.

1. Pray to God daily.

2. Read the Injeel.
   The Holy Injeel is the word of God. It is food for your spiritual life.

3. Obey God's commandments in the Injeel.

4. Testify to others in word and deed, of what God has done in your life.

5. Fellowship with other believers. It is important to fellowship with other individuals who made the same commitment to follow Jesus Christ.

If you have accepted the Christian "Adha" and seek an in-depth study of the teachings of Christ, write to:

Crescent Project
P.O. Box 50986
Indianapolis, IN 46250

RESPONSE FORM

❏ I have received Jesus Christ as my Savior.

❏ I would like a copy of the Injeel.
   Language preference:_____

❏ I would like an in-depth study of the teachings of Christ.

Name_____

Address_____

City_____

State_____

Zip_____

Country_____

Phone _____

Complete form and mail to:
Crescent Project
P.O. Box 50986
Indianapolis, IN 46250
www.crescentproject.org/resourcesformuslims

Or email:
info@crescentproject.org

إن كنت قد قبلت الأضحى وتريد أن تدرس تعاليم المسيح في الإنجيل. أرسل هذه القسيمة :

الأسم: _____

العنوان: _____

_____

الهاتف: _____

Crescent Project
P.O. Box 50986
Indianapolis, IN 46250
www.crescentproject.org/resourcesformuslims
info@crescentproject.org

نقاط للنمو الروحي

إنَّ قبول المسيح كالمخلص والسيد على حياتك هو بداية حياة جديدة مع الله. نقترح عليك بعض النقاط للنمو الإنجيلي.

1. صلِّ يوميًا - الصلاة هي محادثة مع الله - الصلاة ممكنة في أي وقت أو مكان - الرب يسمع دعاك.

2. اقرأ الإنجيل المقدس: الإنجيل المقدس هو كلمة الله وهي كغذاء لحياتنا الروحية.

3. أطع الله يوميًا في حياتك.

4. اشهد للآخرين بالقول والعمل عن خلاص الله في حياتك.

5. اشترك مع مؤمنين آخرين في درس الإنجيل والصلاة. من المهم أن تكون لك شركة مع مؤمنين آخرين، الذين اتبعوا المسيح عيسى.

صل هذه الصلاة واطلب من المسيح أن يدخل حياتك ويغفر خطاياك ويصلح علاقتك بالله. إن طلبت بإخلاص من المسيح أن يدخل حياتك، تأكد بأنه فعل كذلك.

<u>من المهم أن تعلم أنّ الله صادق وأمين</u>

الإنجيل صريح بالتأكيد أن المسيح عيسى أمين في مواعيده.
قال المسيح: «لا أهملك ولا أتركك.» (عبرانيين 13: 5)

«المسيح هو هو، أمسًا واليوم وإلى الأبد.»
(عبرانيين 13: 8)

«إنني عالم بمن آمنت وموقن أنه قادر أن يحفظ وديعتي.» (2تيموثاوس 1: 12)

الصلاة بحسب الإنجيل هي محادثه مع الله، يمكننا التحدث مع الله في أي وقت وفي أي مكان.

يمكنك قبول تضحية المسيح الآن بالصلاة إلى الله بإيمان (أي بثقة في مواعيد الله).

نقترح عليك هذا الدعاء:

«يا رب، يا أرحم الراحمين، أشكرك لأجل محبتك وخلاصك. إني أتوب عن خطاياي وأشهد أن المسيح هو الفادي الوحيد. اغفر لي إكرامًا لتضحية المسيح، أنا أقبل المسيح مخلصًا وسيدًا لحياتي. اجعلني إنسانًا جديدًا. أشكرك لأنك أعطيتني حياة أبدية. باسم المسيح أصلي. آمين».

»لأنكم بالنعمة مخلَّصون بالإيمان وذلك ليس منكم، هو عطية الله. ليس من أعمال كيلا يفتخر أحد«
(الإنجيل المقدس، أفسس 2: 8-9)

علينا قبول هدية الله لكي نتنعم بها. نحن نقبل عمل المسيح بقرار شخصي.

المسيح يود قيادة حياتنا وتطهيرنا من كل أثم وتوطيد الطريق بيننا وبين الله سبحانه وتعالى. يريد المسيح أن يكون مخلِّصًا وسيدًا على حياتنا. يقول المسيح في الإنجيل المقدس:
»أنا واقف على الباب وأقرع، إن سمع أحد صوتي وفتح الباب، أدخل إليه وأتعشى معه.« (رؤيا 3: 20)

لنحصل على الخلاص من خطايانا، علينا أن نتوب عنها ونشهد أن المسيح هو الفادي والمخلِّص الوحيد.

الله يغفر خطايانا لأنّ المسيح كان فاديًا للبشرية، والغفران يجوز لأن عدل الله قد استوفي. لقد ظهرت رحمة الله في الأضحى الإنجيلي.

الإنسان يحتاج لعملية زرع قلب جديد وفكر جديد. قلب جديد مع حياة جديدة تُحوِّل الإنسان الخاطئ إلى إنسان بار.

فداء المسيح أعتقنا من سلطان الخطية والموت.

إن هبة الله هي الحياة الأبدية في قبول تضحية المسيح.

نحن نقبل تضحية المسيح بالإيمان (أي الثقة بمواعيد الله). تضحية المسيح لا تُقدَّر بثمن؛ نقبلها بالإيمان، إذ لا نقدر أن نقدم شيئًا بالمقابل.

5— الإنجيل يعلم أن الله غفور

لا يكفي أن نعرف أنَّ الله وجد كفارة لخطايانا، بل على كلٍّ منا أن يقبل هذه الكفارة بقرار شخصي متواضع. علينا أن نتوب عن خطايانا ونقبل المسيح كمخلّص وسيّد لحياتنا.

التوبة هي التحوّل من الذات إلى الله وإطاعته. التوبة هي الحصول على غفران الله لخطايانا إكرامًا لعمل المسيح الكفاري على الصليب (الأضحى الإنجيلي).

أنزل في الإنجيل:
«إن اعترفنا بخطايانا فهو أمين وعادل حتى يغفر لنا خطايانا ويطهرنا من كل إثم» (1 يوحنا 1: 9).

جميع أعمال الإنسان الصالحة لا تقاس بصلاح الله وقداسته وبره. لا يمكن لأحد أن يعوّض عن خطاياه بأعمال صالحة بشرية محدودة. لأن الخطية هي بحق الله وشريعته.

أرسل الله المسيح ليكون كفارة عن خطايانا. المسيح هو الأضحى الحقيقي. الأضحى الإنجيلي حاضر لجميع الناس لأن المسيح جاء ليخلص جميع البشر. المسيح هو الجسر الذي يمكِّننا من العبور فوق هوة الخطية لنعبد الله في شركة واختبار لمحبته وقداسته.

المسيح هو حمل الله القدوس الذي رفع خطية العالم وبنى جسرًا فوق هوة الخطية التي تفصلنا عن الله وعن محبته وقداسته.

أنزل في الإنجيل المقدس:
«الله كان في المسيح مصالحًا العالم لنفسه غير حاسب لهم خطاياهم.» (2كورنثوس 5: 18)

في خلاصة هذا التأمل والتمعن في تعاليم الإنجيل، نجد أن المسيحيين يحتفلون بعيد الأضحى والفصح معًا في الذكرى المجيدة لموت وقيامة سيدنا المسيح عيسى. و هذا الاحتفال يُعرف بعيد القيامة.

إن حادثتَي الأضحى والفصح هما دروس تحضيرية لكي يفهم الإنسان عمل المسيح الكفاري على الصليب. «بدون سفك دم لا تحصل مغفرة»، المسيح هو الأضحى الحقيقي.

الخلاص والرحمة يمكن الحصول عليهما؛ حين يدفع الثمن. وكما فدى الله ابن إبراهيم بكبش عجيب؛ هكذا فدى الله العالم أجمع بالمسيح عيسى بن مريم.

المسلمون يضحون بذبيحة في عيد الأضحى. واليهود يضحون بذبيحة في عيد الفصح. هكذا فدى الله البشرية بالذبيحة العظمى المسيح عيسى.

الأضحى الحقيقي والفصح الحقيقي هو المسيح عيسى فادي البشرية جمعاء.

المسيح كان حمل الله الذي أزال خطية العالم.

قال يوحنا المعمدان، المعروف أيضًا بيحيا النبي، «هوذا حمل الله الذي يرفع خطية العالم» (بشارة يوحنا 1: 29)

عجيبًا في موته وقيامته

لم يأت المسيح إلى العالم فقط لصنع المعجزات وهدى العالمين، بل أتى لخلاص الإنسان. المسيح هو الفادي الذي مات عن الإنسان دافعًا أجرة الخطية وقام من الموت لأجل خلاصنا.

المسيح بار وطاهر منذ ولادته. «لم يفعل خطية ولا وجد في فمه مكر.» المسيح هو البار الذي يفدي الأثمة. لا يمكن لخاطئ أن يفدي خاطئًا آخر من عقاب الموت. ولكن المسيح بار وموته عوضًا عنا يحقق عدل الله.

«المسيح مات من أجل خطايانا حسب الكتب. ودفن وقام في اليوم الثالث حسب الكتب.»
(الإنجيل المقدس 1 كورنثوس 15: 3).

إن ولادة المسيح ليس من مشيئة إنسان بل من مشيئة الله. إن المسيح فريد في ولادته ومميّز عن جميع الأنبياء والرسل.

جميع الأنبياء والرسل أقروا أنهم مجرد بشر عاديين ولكن المسيح أعلن أنه هو كلمة الله المتجسد. إن الله على كل شيء قدير وهذه المعجزة مدونة في الإنجيل في بشارة لوقا الإصحاح 2 آيات 3-7.

حياة خارقة

عاش المسيح حياة قداسة وطهارة وأطاع أمر الله في كل حياته. كان هو روح الحق ولم يكن في فمه غش. لم يفعل الخطية بل بالحري عمل وعلّم كل ما أمر به الله. أقام الموتى وشفى المرضى وعمل المعجزات. لقد كان المسيح أعظم معلم عرفه التاريخ.

4- الإنجيل يعلّم أن الله رحوم

شاء الله برحمته الواسعة أن يجد حلاً لهذه المعضلة لأنّ الله يود الشركة مع الإنسان ولكن الخطية فاصلة بيننا وبينه. فقط الإنسان الطاهر يقدر أن يقف في الثغر ويسد هذه الهوة. ولكن الإنجيل يقول إنَّ «الجميع أخطأوا.» الجميع ما عدا المسيح عيسى ابن مريم!

الإنجيل يعلِّم أن المسيح هو روح الحق والعلاج الوحيد لهذه المعضلة. وهو الجسر فوق هوة الخطية الذي يعيد الشركة بين الله القدوس والإنسان الخاطئ.

لماذا المسيح وليس إنسانًا آخر؟

ولادته العجيبة
لم يكن للمسيح أب بشري ولكنه حُبل به بقوة الروح القدس في أحشاء مريم العذراء، وهو الإنسان الوحيد الذي ولد من عذراء.

الإنسان خاطئ ولا يقدر أن يرضي قداسة الله وعدله.

يظن البعض أن عملاً صالحًا يغفر عملاً باطلاً. وعلى سبيل المثال، لنفرض أنك طلبت مني الحفاظ على منزلك وأنت في سفر. وعند رجوعك وجدت السيارة نظيفة والبيت مرتبًا ولكن بعض الأثاث مخرب. هل تنظيف البيت يعوّض عن أثاث المنزل؟ من يدفع ثمن أثاث جديد؟ هل يجوز مسامحتي فقط لأني طلبت الغفران؟ إن غفرت لي وسامحتني فمن سيعوض بأثاث جديد؟

إن الأعمال الصالحة واجب علينا ولا يجوز مقايضتها للتكفير عن خطايانا، لأن الله عادل وحكيم ومنزه عن الخطأ. «أجرة الخطية موت» والخاطئ ملزم بدفع الثمن و العقاب.

إن عدالة الله تحتم معاقبة الخطية وأتباعها. انزل في الإنجيل المقدس: «أجرة الخطية هي موت.» لا يجوز لخاطئ محكوم عليه بالموت أن يموت بدل خاطئ آخر. لا يمكن لمجرم أن يفدي مجرمًا آخر لأن العدل يجزم بتنفيذ القصاص على المجرم.

إن خطايانا هي في حق الله عز وجل، لذلك فالعدالة تحتم دفع الثمن والعقاب. على سبيل المثال: إن سرق الإنسان مبلغ ألف درهم، عليه أن يرد ألف درهم. لا أقل ولا أكثر. إن أخطأنا بحق الله، ماذا ندفع مقابل خطئنا؟ إن أعمالنا الصالحة لا توازي ولا تضاهي صلاح الله وقداسته.

الإنسان عاجز عن إرضاء الله بأعماله الخيرة لأنها أعمال بالية ومحدودة إذا ما قارناها بالله وبعظمته وبقداسته، سبحانه وتعالى.

إن خطية الإنسان هي اختيار الإرادة الذاتية العنيدة وعصيان شريعة الله. هذا العصيان يدعوه الإنجيل خطية والخطية هي الفاصل بين الله والإنسان.

3— الإنجيل يعلم أن الله عادل

إن خطية الإنسان هي الفاصل بينه وبين محبة الله وقداسته. قداسة الله تدين الخطية. قداسة الله لا تقبل الخطية أبدًا. فلذلك هناك هوة عظيمة بين الله القدوس والإنسان الخاطئ. ولا يمكن لخاطئ أن يفدي خاطئًا آخر.

بسبب هذه الهوة العظيمة، انقطعت الشركة مع الله فأصبح الإنسان بلا هدف.

لإنارة المنزل نحتاج إلى الضوء وقوة الكهرباء. بدون الكهرباء يبقى الضوء (اللمبة) بلا هدف ولا قوة. هكذا الإنسان بدون الشركة مع الله هو ميت روحيًا وبلا هدف.

2— الإنجيل يعلم أن الله قدوس

الله قدوس والإنسان خاطئ وكيفما توجهنا نجد خطايا البشرية. وأعمال الإنسان الخاطئة ما هي إلا عوارض لداء يدعى الخطية. الخطية هي عصيان الله وجعل حياتنا معتمدة على نفوسنا وقدرتنا وأرادتنا. الإنسان عصى الله وأخطأ بحق الله جاعلاً هوة بينه وبين الله القدوس. لا يمكن لله القدوس أن يكون في شركة مع الإنسان الخاطئ. لا شركة بين الظلمة والنور. لا يمكن أن يكون نهار وليل في وقت واحد.

الإنجيل يشدد على أن جميع الناس أخطأوا.
(رومية 3: 10-11)

الإنجيل يؤكد أن «أجرة الخطية هي موت، أما هبة الله فهي حياة أبدية.» (رومية 3: 23).

1- الإنجيل يعلّم أنّ الله محب

الله سبحانه وتعالى، خالق السموات والأرض وكل ما فيها؛ شاء من خلق الكون والإنسان أن يتمتع في شركة خاصة مع الإنسان. الإنسان هو ذروة الخليقة ويتمتع بالعقل والإرادة. الله محب وعطوف نحو خليقته.

أنزل في الإنجيل:

«الله محبة ومن يثبت في المحبة يثبت في الله.» رسالة يوحنا الأولى 4: 16

قال المسيح عيسى:

«أتيت لتكون لهم حياة ولتكون حياة أفضل.»
بشارة يوحنا 10: 10

بما أن الله عز وجل يريد الشركة مع الإنسان، لماذا عالمنا بعيد عن إطاعة الله وشريعته؟ يبدو وكأن هوة كبيرة تفصل بين الله والإنسان مانعة الإنسان من محبة الله و التمتع بها.

ويحتفل اليهود سنويًا بعيد الفصح. حادثة الفصح مذكورة في التوراة في سفر الخروج إصحاح 12 آيات 1-14.

ولكن أين الأضحى المسيحي؟
المسيحيون يؤمنون بحادثتي الأضحى والفصح، ولكن لماذا لا يحتفلون بعيد خاص للأضحى وعيد خاص للفصح؟
هل هناك فصح مسيحي أيضًا؟
للإجابة عن هذه الأسئلة، علينا أن نتمعّن في رسالة الإنجيل ونتأمّل في صفات الرب عز وجل.

ونظر إبراهيم ووجد كبشًا معلقًا فأخذه وقدّمه ذبيحة لله. هذه الحادثة مدوّنة في التوارة وفي سفر التكوين إصحاح 22 آيات 1-19.

الديانة اليهودية لا تحتفل في هذه المناسبة بعيد خاص ولكن معناها مضمون في عيد الفصح. عيد الفصح هو احتفال بذكرى فداء أبكار أنفس الإسرائيليين في مصر. أمَرَ الله ملاك الموت العبور عن كل من وضع دم الذبيحة على قوام باب المنزل والاقتصاص من كل بكر ذكر من عائلات مصر.

أمَر النبي موسى بذبح حمل ووضع دمه على عتبة المنزل العليا. كل من وضع دم الذبيحة على مدخل المنزل عبر عنه ملاك الموت، وبهذا ينجو الابن البكر.

الأضحى في الإنجيل

يحتفل المسلمون سنويًا بعيد الأضحى في العاشر من ذو الحجّة. الأضحى مشتقة من اسم الضحية وتعني ذبيحة لله. عيد الأضحى يُدعى العيد الكبير وأيضًا يدعى «قرباني» في نواحي بلاد الأتراك.

يحتفل المسلمون بعيد الأضحى بذكرى خلاص ابن إبراهيم حين كان على وشك أن يقدّمه ذبيحة لله. وهذه الحادثة ذكرت في سورة الصافات آيات 99-111.

الديانة اليهودية تؤمن بهذه الحادثة المجيدة لأن الله فدى ابن إبراهيم بكبش عجيب. أنزل في التوراة أن الملاك أوقف إبراهيم حين كان على وشك أن يذبح ابنه وقال له: «لا تفعل!» (تكوين 22: 12)